SECRET LINES

MAHUNA H RAPHALA

FACEBOOK: PURE PAGE PRES

AND/OR

SECRET LINES POETRY

LOVE IS JOYOUS

September 2017

ISBN-13: 978 0 620 76500 8
ISBN-10: 0620765003

LOVE IS JOYOUS

DEDICATION

Dedicated to myself, my brothers and sisters, my mother, my entire extended family, my friends and to my LATE father, MAY HIS SOUL REST IN PEACE. A poem titled tribute to my late father is attached; however the lines are not visible for they are a secret in my heart, hence, SECRET LINES.

LOVE IS MISERABLE

CONTENTS

SONNETS

ACKNOWLEDGMENTS

Everyone who has been supportive of my writing, thank you very much for the inspiration, God bless you all.

FOREWORD

"Day dreaming" explains my journey in writing. It is not merely a fantasy I had about the woman of my dreams. The title itself outlines a vision and not a definite dream because it is daylight. The first line outlines the thoughts that were in my mind, where they were making noise because I could not stop thinking. The second line talks about being in dreams, and that actually adds flavour to the fact of thoughts. It means that I was away from the real world, but in my own world trying to find my calling. The third line mentions the type of the dream, which is a very scary one. It surely was not a nightmare, but it seemed to be a huge dream that is very superior to my abilities. The forth line outlines altercation with thugs. This is the point where I was not sure if I will be able to achieve the goal I am setting for myself. I questioned my weaknesses and strengths. The fifth line highlights the purpose of the dream. It wasn't a woman like the poem says.

The "woman of my dreams" in this case was actually my "writing". The sixth line talks about waking up, which in this sense is when I wanted to stop about these hallucinations of myself being a writer. As the seventh line says I tried to stand up, is when I told myself that I am going to do it, one way or another. With the eighth line, my fears shot me to death and I started to doubt my abilities of writing. But the ninth line says "I was not yet dead", this means I still had some hope and I decided that against all odds I am going for it. The tenth line talks about stealing, which is my fears that wanted to take my dream away from me. And the eleventh line says "but I put them to stop", which outlines the fact that I looked at the bigger picture and forgot about all the negativities. The twelfth line "before I could realize", outlines that I didn't see it coming, furthermore with the thirteenth line "the property was released", I found myself writing and doing well unconsciously. The last line talks about being released from the dreams, which is writing in reality and no longer fantasies.

LOVE IS MISERABLE

LOVE AT FIRST SIGHT

I still remember the day we met
The day I got joy in my heart
The very same day I felt like a man
For the first time in my life

And probably the last time of my life
You were standing aside with your friends
And I was sitting there at the corner all alone
Fantasizing my life with you

I Felt love running through my veins
When I looked at you, and you looked at me
I was embarrassed but your smile made me
Feel like I am in heaven

Because I thought,
You will only smile at me on my fantasies
Yet I was very wrong, I could not believe my eyes
But it was happening in reality, not in wonderland

And I knew for sure that the first step
Of confessing my love to you was imposed
When I called you, your friends seemed so sure
Of what I wanted to tell you

Maybe that's why they convinced you to hear my story
The first word that came from your mouth
Made me even more embarrassed and shy
But when you smiled

Your white teeth glittered like gold
Then I was able to say my part
The rapid change that was on your face
Made me more nervous

I thought you would react negatively
But when you touched me and held my hand, I nearly froze
When you told me that you have been watching me
As much as I did, I nearly collapsed

Until you told me that you love me
And my memory went blank
Where my heart Skipped a beat and I thought, I was dying
Unaware of the affection between us

I fell in love with you the very first second I saw your face
It was as if I can see through your chest
Seeing my name engraved on your heart
The Lord created you very specially for me

And I promise to hold on to you
No matter how hard or sweet it can be
You will forever be painted on my heart
In my mind, and in my soul

RAPHALA MH©

FELL FOR YOU

I just happened to love you
I did not mean to put you under pressure
I tried to resist but I love you
By just seeing you, my heart pleasures

I made peace that I will not confess
Because I respect you enough
To go through this process
But I also love you enough

That I can no longer live with lies
I know I did not come clean in time
But in my heart your soul lies
I will keep you warm forever at all times

I promise to love you everyday
I wish we can be together forever
For all our years and days
On this planet forever more

I promise to not hurt you
Because to me you mean so much more
That I even fail to tell how much I love you
If I could write a book

About my love for you
It will not be just any book
It would be titled the special you
And the content will melt

One's memory and fail to interpret
Because loving you is not what I just felt

LOVE IS JOYOUS

And it is also not an entertainment
It comes from the centre of my heart

It travels along the veins with blood
It hits my entire body cells hard
As my blood runs like floods
Forgive me for loving you

It was not by choice
But I cannot stop loving you
Even if I had a choice
I wish you could understand

I wish not to stress you
But it can be hard for you to understand
Because I really, and conditionally love you
The condition is, for as long as I live

I will love you forever
The condition will forever live
In my heart, so that I love you forever
I am not trying to impress

Nor outplay you
But rather I express
My feelings for you
I would never lie about my feelings

Especially to a special woman like you
But believe me; I know what I am feeling
Every love particle in me sings you
Be my love

And I will be yours
Then we can define true love

LOVE IS MISERABLE

And make it ours
It all happens in the name of love

Because I so much love you
And I want to be with you

RAPHALA MH©

THE CRUELTY OF LOVE

Love hurts when you think you have it
When you think you love someone
Only to find out that it was just emotions
When you really believe that you are in love
Only to realize that you were fooling yourself

The moment you realize that
Things are bad, they are worse
What hurts most is that you were never loved
You were only made to believe that you are loved
The pain penetrates deep into your heart

Because you really believed that you are loved
Yet you were played
But that did not stop you
From really loving your player
The saddest thing is that there is absolutely

Nothing you can do about it
And you just have to let go
The pains of being in infatuation
Where there is no medication
That is the cruelty of love

RAPHALA MH©

LOVE IS MISERABLE

IGNORANCE

I should have known
That she would ignore me
Yet I had no knowledge
That ignorance can hurt me

I know she did not literally mean
To break my heart
Because her heart is not mean
She has a sweetheart

That's why I love her
I wish she could
Let me be with her
Only if she could

Know how much love
I have for her
Maybe she will love
Me and let me be with her

I wish she could realize
At an early stage
So that I will still be at reach
Because at some stage

Life can happen
That I lose interest
But I pray it does not occur
Because I cannot afford to lose interest

On someone I love so much
It will all tear me apart

LOVE IS JOYOUS

That no one can ever rematch
The puzzles that are scattered apart

They will be representing my heart
That would be bleeding
Because it would really be hurt
By someone who is beautiful

With no intensions of hurting me
I wish she could let me
Be with her in not any type of love
For the rest of our lives being in real love

RAPHALA MH©

THAT MOMENT

That moment when you are sitting all alone
Thinking that you are relaxing
Trying to reminisce or planning your future ahead
Fantasizing about something good
Having fun in your own land

Then something swiftly crosses your mind
And it unfortunately takes your full attention
That woman you really love
Who probably doesn't even know that
But what if she knows

It hurts if she doesn't want to be with you
For reasons that only and only her knows
What hurts most is that she can't
Or rather won't cough it out
Why she can't be with you

That moment when you talk to her
And her response drives your nerves
Carrying love impulse
Directly to the core of your heart
Like a railway drives a train straight to the station

The saddest thing about this situation
Is that you are told that the two of you cannot
And will never be together
What hurts even worse is that
You are told that there's nothing you can do

To make the two of you to be together
Yet, the two of you really love each other

LOVE IS JOYOUS

Even if she doesn't want to admit it
She'd rather conceal her visible
And transparent feelings

That even a blind man can see
Reality is, "that moment hurts"
The pain is unbearable
That it even makes you miserable
And you have to forget about everything

RAPHALA MH©

LOVE IS MISERABLE

DANCE BY YOUR TUNE

There is at least one thing I know
I will always be by your side
I will always say yes to you
Even when I am right
I will concur with you to make you right

I will take the downfall of being wrong
I will always apologise to make you right
Even when you are wrong
I will let you win every altercation
I will let you be the master mind

The controller of our relationship
No matter what, I will always
Sacrifice for your happiness
Even at the expense of mine
I will let you be the puppet master

And I will settle to being the puppet
I grant you permission to be the coach
And I will be the player
I wish you can be coach of the season
So that I'll be the player of the season

I give you my heart fully
And you can control my life
You are the guitarist and I am the dancer
I will be obedient to you, no matter what
I will always dance by your tune

Not because I have no choice
I do have a choice

I believe I made the right one
I chose to love you
I let you to rule my love for you

Adjust it to the level you want
Because I have enough love for you
And for you only
I will always dance by your tune
Even when you play off tune

RAPHALA MH©

LOVING A CRUSH

I always dream to be with you
I always fantasize
About you and I being in a relationship
But all that fades away in just a few seconds
You are not just a crush

You are the woman I really adore
The one and the only one I love most
I usually say, only if you felt how much I love you
Then you will definitely know the meaning of my love to you
But it is more like waiting for an aeroplane at the train station

I try by all means to describe my love for you
But that seems impossible because every time I do it I get
hurt
And my mind goes blank then I become blind
But blind in love
I love you, the Lord is my witness

At times I wish God could send you angels
To let you know how much I love you
People usually advise me to give up and move on
But that's like a train moving forward and leaving its coaches
behind
If I move on, it has to be with you, or there will be no
moving on

If I was a pastor, I would preach about you
If I was a doctor, I would use your names as medical terms
If I was a teacher, I would definitely teach about you
And no learner of mine would fail

If I was a scientist, I would discover laws and principles about you

If I was a mathematician, I would derive formulas about you
But because I am an ordinary me
I'll always love you unconditionally
That people would even be able to derive
The meaning of true love from "our love"

There are billions of beautiful girls in this world
But amongst them all
I love you, and I choose to be with you only
That makes you extra special
Even when I see beautiful girls

I always ignore and have less interest on them
Because I love you and I always hope that one day
You will consider my love and we will be together
Until death separates us
I love you a lot; you are not just a crush

RAPHALA MH©

COMMITTED TO MY CRUSH

I don't care what other people think or say
I only care about you
Because you are special
You are the only one that makes me feel
Like an extra ordinary person
For that I really love you

I hurt someone
So deeply that I would not want
Anyone to hurt me the way I did
Yes I did not want to
But somehow I had to
That certain someone is a woman
Who really loves me
I don't know how much
But definitely she extremely loves me

I can say this because she was brave
Enough to propose to me
It was like a dream
Because I was never proposed
By a girl before
She was the first one to be brave
Such that she was able to let me
Know how she feels about me

I was not surprised though
Because she gave me signs before she could propose
She probably saw through me that I didn't give her much
interest
So she just coughed it out, poor girl

LOVE IS JOYOUS

I hurt her deeply because I rejected her offer
It was more like I don't care what you feel
I know I was being cruel by not at least trying
But my intentions could not let me
I was and still not intended to be with her
Nor anybody else, except someone
She probably thinks that I am too mean
Or rather unkind, but at least she knows better
It's clear and simply obvious that she studied me
Before she could actually make a move
And she cannot go for someone who is mean and unkind

I love someone
I am deeply in love with my crush
Damn I rejected her for my crush
Did I make a wise move, or was I really cruel
But I love my crush like nobody's business
I don't even care what one thinks
Because my love for her is not conditional
Irrespective of her imperfections, I love her more

The only problem is that she cannot see my love for her
Only if she could gauge it
Perhaps she would be more than a crush to me
She does know that I love her
And she is not rejecting me
But she's also not accepting me instantaneously
How surprising is it
Only she can answer that
Despite everything
I AM COMMITTED TO MY CRUSH!!!

RAPHALA MH©

LOVE IS MISERABLE

AFFECTION

Love is the most powerful feeling
That tends to control ones thinking
The feeling is mutual in nature
Although people abuse it
Those who are in real love

Are usually berserk in thinking
Love drives people to do unpleasant things
That makes them to regret later
The main issue is affection
We usually love those we can't be with

Such people are usually really loved in fantasies
Because we fear reality
We are with them from far
But we are in fact far from being with them
Because we usually fail to tell them as it is never easy

The problem associated with affection
Is that we do things conditionally
To satisfy a particular feeling
We will be feeling at that particular moment
We propose to other women

Forgetting about our women at that moment
But we always regret later
When we miss our women
We sometimes feel emotional
And propose to other women

Frequent contact with a certain woman
Might make you have a crush on her
It is difficult to take a decision

LOVE IS JOYOUS

Or rather action after realizing the mistake made
But sometimes affection is not a mistake
What if you develop more feelings
For that crush of yours
Then you eventually tend to really love her

RAPHALA MH©

SOUL PROVIDER

One thing I would do when I am bored
Is to think about something special
Something that makes me feel good
Something that turns my dark days
Into a more lighter one

Anything that makes me sad or depressed
Can be converted into happiness and smiles
When I am too low, I know which element
Will make me feel better
This element always makes me feel like

I am up in the sky
This element is not in the periodic table
But it is very special on its own
When life throws storms at me
They are turned into manna

When life throws thunder storms at me
They are turned into light
That shows me the way forward
For every obstacle I encounter
A bridge is constructed on top of it

So that I can pass through
For any form of adversity
Is turned into a path for success
Any negative thought in my mind
Is turned into a positive one

Any negative energy and attitude in me
Is manipulated into a ladder for success

For when my soul is weak
She provides me with a stronger one
All because she is my soul provider

RAPHALA MH©

SMILE

A smile represents happiness
It wears away sadness
It starts a good conversation
And it can also be an introduction
It creates a happy environment
As it makes one feel like an ornament
It is also a simple of love
And goes hand in hand with laugh
It's a way of showing attention
And acts as an attention retention
It opens many doors
And picks up one from the floor
It makes one feel good
As if they are having soul food
It is the foundation of loving
By a way of flirting
As it can prevent crying
And creates laughing
It is a token of appreciation
And can also create affection
It keeps one going
Even when they are hurting
It never hurts
But it can bless
It clears away ugliness
And promotes adorableness
It can nurture
And it is beautiful in nature

RAPHALA MH ©

STILL REMEMBER

I still remember
The first time I fell in love
How it happened I don't remember
I didn't know how to love
But I had a different feeling
That I had never felt my entire life
I guess I was driven by feelings
And that changed my life
Because I learned how to love
I was on top of my game
When it comes to love
I don't play silly games
I give it my all
I let my heart to really love
Very hard like a wall
I enjoy being in love
I don't care about being hurt
Because I trust my love
It is strong enough to sooth a heart
That is the real love
If I can find a partner
Whom she really loves me
We can be the best partners
That from she and I
People can define true love
As we will be defining it

RAPHALA MH©

LOVE IS MISERABLE

LUST IS NOT LOVE

If you feel like loving
But your heart does not force
Out your feelings
Do not use force
You are not in love
Stop torturing yourself
Let your heart find love
To prevent yourself
From being hurt
Or rather hurting
Someone's soul
And create a hole
Deep inside their heart
Because you would have hurt
Them too deep
Because of lust
You can also feel
That it was never love
Lusting someone
Can also hurt someone
Because you don't really love
The innocent person whom may love
You a lot in return
Fully expressing a feeling you can't return
Just respect yourself
And your beautiful heart
You will be saving yourself
From hurting a beautiful heart

RAPHALA MH ©

NEED SOMEBODY TO LOVE

I need someone I can express myself to
I need the right person to love
Love is burning inside me
I just need someone to pass it to
My heart is bleeding, for it overworks
It pumps the blood and stores too much love

I just need that somebody to offload my love to
My body is burning with love
Every cell in me carries love impulse
It leaves with my blood from the heart
Through my veins it travels to all parts of the body
It seems like I will suffocate, because I lack oxygen

All because the air that I inhale
Is concentrated with love
When I exhale, no love is present in the exhaled air
I am about to go crazy because it accumulates in my mind
I fail to think well sometimes, because all I think of is the
love in my cerebrum
My mind fails to interpret information because of the
concentrated love

My vision is gradually degenerating
Because all I see is love
My hearing is also deteriorating
All because the only sound I access is love
I need that someone whom I can love
So that my vision and hearing can regenerate back to normal

Only if I could have somebody to love
Then my optic and auditory canal can be lubricated
My central nervous system is also under construction
And needs that somebody to love so that I can be renovated

LOVE IS MISERABLE

My cardiovascular system needs a lover, to set my heart and veins free
I need somebody to love, so that my respiratory tract can be unblocked

When I smell, only love enters my nasal passage
I can't differentiate between different smells anymore
When I touch, I feel like I am touching an untouchable feeling
My taste buds are fixed to taste love
I am always feeling love in every particle of my body
All my sensations are linked to love

I need somebody to love
So that my sensations can function normally again
I just have enough love in me
Waiting for not anybody
But a special somebody to love
I NEED SOMEBODY TO LOVE

RAPHALA MH©

BEEN WAITING

I went up and down
Trying to find love
From nights to dawns
I could not see love

I've been with many partners
Hoping to find the right one
All of them seemed to be starters
They were never in the game even once

They all tried not to hurt
But they don't know how to love
At the end I end up being hurt
Then people have a reason to laugh

I tried to find love
But I failed many times
I found those who try to love
But our love sublimed

I've been knocking at many doors
But many times I hit the floor
I tried to jump into the love train
But I couldn't hold onto the same rail

I had lost hope on love
Feeling like I'll never be loved
I tried to remain single
But everything was just mingled

My heart no longer had feelings
And it required healing

LOVE IS MISERABLE

But I could no longer feel pains
For pains on my heart were painted

My blood stream was full of hatred
But with time, that faded
At the beginning it was nothing
But later it became a special something

After all the waiting
And all the wanting
I finally found something
A more extra ordinary thing

I've been waiting for you all along
You brought life to the spirit of love
I've been waiting for too long
But at the end I found real love

You made me believe in love again
Although I've been hurt
And I'll never be hurt again
Because there is joy in my heart

A precious gift I got
For I met you sweetheart
I thank God
For soothing my heart

Not so long ago
My heart was torn apart
I even lost my ego
My life fell apart

But then I met you
And everything changed
I'll never lose you
And that will never change

LOVE IS JOYOUS

A promise I paint on your heart
That I'll forever be yours
And you will never be hurt
For I will hold on to being yours

No matter the circumstances
And all the obstacles
I will always love you
Because I was made for you

Thank you for loving me
I thought I was getting old
But you changed me
For I've been waiting for too long

RAPHALA MH ©

I LOVE HER

She is not just a woman
Yes, she is beautiful
She makes me feel like a man
Not because of her beauty
She is very unique

I think of her daily
She is like an antique
Her value increases daily
We did not grow up together
We met a few years ago

We luckily went to school together
But it feels like I have known her for a while ago
I did not fall in love with her at the first instinct
We became friends unconsciously
But I fell for her instantly

And that happened consciously
I tried to resist
I was tied up by another woman
But I could feel my feelings persist
As I gradually detached from a woman

To whom I thought we were in love
But I was hurt deeply
And finally I found my love
Whom I love so deeply
A very special being she is to me

I do not have her already
But the little she is giving me

LOVE IS JOYOUS

Makes me very ready
That when and if she opens
I would give it my all

I appreciate the little I get
And I want to keep it all to my heart
So that when times gets
Tough and situations intensifies
I know that it will keep me going

And I am ready to sacrifice
Anything to keep us going
If loving her is a dream
Then please don't wake me up
I would rather remain in dreams

Than to give it all up
If loving her is a crime
I would rather be a prisoner
Even if I had pride
I would still love her being a prisoner

RAPHALA MH ©

LOVE IS MISERABLE

I AM FREE

I am now a free being
I enjoy being single
I won't be hurt for any reason being
My life is no longer mingled
No one will hurt my feelings
For I am not a unit
I know how good I am feeling
I therefore require no unity
To be in love with someone
Who will make me feel unwanted
For I won't be depending on anyone
Because being single is what I wanted
Not because of circumstances
And it feels good
Because there are no love obstacles
That prevents my life to be rated good
I am not on sale
I am not looking for a partner
I am happy as one soul
Living happily without a partner
That would probably hurt me
I've no one to fight with
Nor no one to play me
I've no one to intimately associate with
And I am living a happy life
I am not feeling lonely
I feel like my heart is free
Not just my heart only
And also my soul
I enjoy my life being solo

RAPHALA MH ©

UNINTENTIONAL LOVE

I did not plan
To fall in love with you
But it is clear and plain
That I really love you
I can't recall how it happened
It was unintentional
But life happened
That I loved you without hesitation
It was an unconditioned response
To the call of nature
I rightfully responded
And it all happened naturally
Every time when the time ticks
I wish I was with you
And I want to stop it from ticking
Because I feel like I am loosing you
I want to hold you tight
Close to my heart
Because I know if you are held tight
I won't lose your heart
It shall forever be mine
And mine will joyously be yours

RAPHALA MH©

LOVE IS MISERABLE

A JOYFUL BEAT

There is a little beat
Pounding hard on my heart
A very special beat
That brings joy to my heart
That sings your name
To all my senses
Love impulses I can name
Because it makes much sense
That I love you with all my particles
I feel and adore you
With all my sensing particles
And I promise you
Baby I will never forsake
Nor forget you ever
Even my love won't forsake
Because I will love you forever
Your heart is mine
They beat simultaneously
It will be a honour for you to be mine
Even if love hurts, ours will heal instantly

RAPHALA MH©

LOVE LETTER

When I look at you
Deep inside your eyes
Fully scanning you
I melt like ice
Because I see a love letter

With no address
But my name appears with capital letters
My love for you is addressed
It got me thinking
Of how much I love you

I know you probably think
That I don't really love you
I probably lust you
But that is not true
And I assure you

I love and I need you, truly
I know you may think
That I am old school
And that you also think
I am not good

Enough to impress
Because I wrote you a letter
But my intention is to express
I can't take the letter
To you myself

Because I can't step on the ladder
Yet I wish to do it myself

LOVE IS MISERABLE

But baby you get me so hot
That I might even burn the envelope
And to have a thought

That my feelings may elope
I just fear facing you
Not because I get scared
I just want to be with you
And forget about the rest

RAPHALA MH©

PROMISE

I know I promised
To unlearn loving you
But it's a tough job
And it gets worse daily

Not better any time soon
But I still promise you
That I will keep my promise
Of doing what makes you happy

And again I will promise
To maintain my promises
No matter the circumstances
I want what is best for you

Yet I need to be with you
I choose to make you happy
It's not about what I need or want
But about what will make you smile

I am not trying to prove a point
And I know things won't change
Overnight like I never loved you
And sometimes I look at your photos

Then I feel very sad and depressed
I feel very angry and betrayed
I feel very much disappointed
I also feel bad, stupid and guilty

And sometimes I do drop a few tears
But then later I smile

LOVE IS MISERABLE

And tell myself that
This beautiful soul deserves better

For if she is very happy
What more could my heart seek
Her happiness is good enough
To make me smile with joy

It's just unfortunate
That it is another man
That makes you smile
And not myself

But I can't take that
Away from you
I adore you very much
To let you go through torture

I'd rather be single
Than taking away your happiness
I'd rather let you be happy
Even at the expense of mine

But either way
I love you so much
And it shall remain as such
For as long as I live

RAPHALA MH©

CAN'T FORGET

I wanted to give up
Forget about everything at once
Take everything up
To the one and only one
Almighty our God
Because I am weak

And I am hurt a lot
A day seems like a week
I can't stop loving you
Although it creates problems
And also that I can't be with you
But that is not a problem

I love you too much
That I even fear
To lose you
It hurts my feelings
That I can't find someone like you
And I have to forget

That you ever existed
But don't forget
That you don't only exist
On this cruel world
But to my heart as well
And you leave holes

They say all will be well
But they don't know the scar
That love left on my heart
They forget that scars

LOVE IS MISERABLE

Are like hats
You forget about them when it's cold
But come hot days

Although they seem old
They remind you of bad dates
They surpass precious memories
Because they have no wounds
For you to keep in your memory
They fade away like fire woods

RAPHALA MH ©

LOVE IS MUTUAL

Love is a mutual thing
It requires two parties
For it to be strong
If one partner is unstable
Then love deteriorates
Even if you love each other
But one does not give their all
Then something is wrong
All because love cannot
Go well with one driver
Two reliable drivers
Must present trust
They must be loyal
And believe in each other
They must stop imposing
Weaknesses and strengths
Of the other partner
They must always show
Some reciprocity to each aspect
They must respect each other
They must forget about negatives
And focus more on positives

RAPHALA MH©

LOVE IS MISERABLE

SPECIAL PLACE

You had a special space crafted
Very special for you in my heart
You were just too blind to see it
You were very selfish to feel it

And very much busy to hear of it
You have crafted you way
You have let it all go my dear
I know I may have tried

Not good enough to express
My feelings to you
But all that is history
I can feel the space closing

It is now smaller than an aisle
You cannot fit into it anymore
Know that time has gone
You are now in the past book

A book that I am about to close
It is too late to love me now
And I hope very much that you don't
Because that will hurt both of us

I am glad you are happy
I am now my own man
Living up to my decisions
And I have decided to move on

Together with my pains and depressions
I just feel for the next person

That I will fall for
And that's if I ever do fall for one

Because you broke my heart
What will I use to fall for someone
If my heart is like trash
Torn into countless pieces

I wish the next person won't have to deal
With the sorrows and pains
Caused by loving you so much as if
Tomorrow was never coming

Only if I had known
I wouldn't have fallen for you
I would have lied to myself rather
I would tell my eyes to never see your beauty

I would have told my soul to never connect to yours
I would have told my heart that you don't exist
But yet I am here
Failing to drown my sorrows

Only God knows I guess
I am sorry for loving you
I wish it was not a mistake
That I loved you so much

RAPHALA MH©

TO LOVE AND HATE

To love and hate at the same time
Is a dangerous game on its own
I should have told you in time
I now feel like I owe
You the truth that hurts
I never wanted to be your friend
But I went against my heart
And pretended as if I am a friend
I actually loved you
A lot more than how I can say it
I should have warned you
But I failed and kept it
Inside my hurting heart
I know it was lame
But I respect your heart
You showed me the lane
And I was ready to make you happy
I didn't care about my feelings
For yourself being happy
Is my greatest feeling
Reality is that I regret
But I chose this life
I wish miracles can happen
That you show me love
Not because you are forced to
And not because you pity me
But because you really do
Want and love me

RAPHALA MH©

LOVE IS JOYOUS

PAINS OF LOVING YOU

For as long as I am living
I will always love you
I am trying to ignore it
But it is destroying me

I can't learn to stop loving you
Because my feelings for you
Are developing everyday
And you are rejecting me everyday

I am indeed experiencing
The cruelty of love to climax
I might as well accept
That I will never find happiness

Being single is my middle name
It hurts to sit back and watch
People take away what I love most
And knowing that I do not

Have the power to do anything
You feel sorry for me
But that will not make me happy
Yet it strengths my love for you

But it seems like I am wasting my love
For nothing but pains and depression
I wonder when you will understand
My love for you at least

Because I am hurting
I am trying to forget about everything

LOVE IS MISERABLE

I need a new hobby
Something that I will enjoy doing

A hobby that would keep me too busy
To even think about you and my problems
The worst problem is that I already found one
And I cannot replace it

I love you so much baby
I am practicing my hobby everyday
I enjoy loving you everyday
It always feels good to love you like this

I always feel happy for thinking
That I love you so much
But I always get hurt for that
At the end of the day

I trust my love
It hurts my heart deeply
But it is strong enough
To also sooth my heart cleanly

RAPHALA MH©

ENOUGH LOVE

I fail to describe
The way I feel about you
It's too much for any human
To really understand my love
A man would say it's impossible

To love someone like this
The only problem is that
We never know what one thinks
Whether one is telling the truth
Can be interpreted

But the answer will
Not be actual or accurate
The chances that
You are really loved
Are there but we never

Know what one feels
My love for you comes at a cost
It is not on sale but it is expensive
I don't know how much it cost
But I know I really love you

The cost may rather
Be the pain you reward me with
As an individual I know how I feel about you
Only if you could feel the same
Perhaps you would know

How much I love you
Empathy is better than sympathy

LOVE IS MISERABLE

I, myself fail to know how much I love you
But at least I know I love you
More than enough

You have the power to
Make me love you
The way you want me to
Simply because I have
Enough love for you

RAPHALA MH©

I WOULD RATHER GO BLIND

I would rather go blind
Than to see you torture me like this
Yet you claim to love me
You still hurt my feelings
You act to be the most caring person
While you are in fact a serpent

I would rather go blind
Than to see you deceive me like this
You tell me to do something
Yet you do the direct opposite
As the greatest hypocrite
Although you are showing signs

That you love me
You disrespect and abuse
Your feelings for me
I would rather go blind
Than to sit back and watch you ruin
The love I have for you

I would rather go blind
Than watching you bring
Sorrows into my life
Time and again
I would rather go blind
Than seeing you abuse me emotionally

You keep a greater distance
Away from me
You are neglecting my love for you
By being an emotional bully

LOVE IS MISERABLE

You are always pushing me away
Yet you claim that we belong together

You enjoy it when I apologize
For things I did not do
Just to make you right
I would rather go blind
Than to see my loving ability
Deteriorate due to your ornery

RAPHALA MH©

UNCLEAR REJECTION

It is fine for you to reject me
I understand because it is natural
For you to hurt me
By clearly rejecting me
Also is very fine
I don't have a problem with you

If you reject me
Because I love you
I understand and value your decisions
Because I love you
I will abide by the instructions
You order me to adhere to

I don't have a problem with you
Playing hard to get
I will understand
Because you know why you are doing it
Although I love you
I will not let you play with my feelings

I will not let you try to control me
Because you think I praise you
Yes I respect you
But you will not order me around
Like your puppet
I will not let you play

With my feelings to that extent
If you reject me, so be it
Even if you don't want what you need
It is fine with me

LOVE IS MISERABLE

Even if you don't know what you want
Rather decide while time still allows you

Or it will be too late
If you want to be with me
Do it before nature changes my mind
I will let you reject me if you want
But let it be a clear rejection
Don't give me a wrong impression

Do not be cold and hot
When the conditions apply
For your benefits
Be with me if you love me
But never ever give me
An unclear rejection

RAPHALA MH©

FAILED TO COUGH OUT

It is not a secret that I love you
Even a blind man can see it
But he cannot measure how much
It is not a mistake that I adore you so much
I chose to get to know you
I chose to be close to you as a friend
But it was not my choice to love you
And I can't stop practicing it
Because I did not even know
That I was loving you until
I started feeling it
When I tried to resist
I loved you even more
When I tried to stop loving you
I became a good lover
Because my feelings for you
Developed even more stronger
I tried to sleep over it until I die
But feelings kept crushing
Inside my hurting heart
Causing me to love you even more
That I even thought we are dating
I eventually came to a decision that
I will confess my love for you
But it was the greatest and hardest task
To ever anticipate in
I adjusted myself to myself
And planned to confess
Small things like seeing you smile
Makes me feel guilty of what I did not do
What I was actually planning to do
The frequent conversations we had

LOVE IS MISERABLE

Made me feel like a king
Because you were always talking like a queen
The hardest thing I failed to do
Was to cough out just three little words
And I didn't know what the future held for us
Until it was too late
Then I realized how much time I've wasted
What kind of love I destroyed before it was built
I failed to cough out I love you
After all it is not an opinion that I love you
It is a definite fact
And the Lord knows it all
Our future is now in the palm of your hands
It's up to you to make us
The happiest couple in the universe
Or destroy what our hearts could build
You have all the power in the world to build us
But also you have the power
To destroy us before
We even construct a foundation
For our love to grow on
Choose to build us
You shall do well in the name of love
But you can also choose
To neglect and destroy us
You shall be immoral
In the name of torture and pains
Whatever happens
Whatever decision you take
I love you baby

RAPHALA MH ©

CAN'T KEEP A DISTANCE

The fact that I love her so much
That I even cry by just thinking about her
Breaks my heart because she doesn't want me
I am trying by all means to adjust to the situation
But that destroys me even worse
I can't get used to the idea

That I really love someone's woman
Who made a choice
Of being with another man over me
I am trying not to think about her
But I cannot do that
I try to stop looking at her

When I am lonely
But still I cannot
I am trying to avoid
My feelings for her
But they develop everyday
I am trying to be just a friend

But I keep on needing more
The more I resist being around her
The more I am attracted to her
The phenomenon that the greater the distance
The less force will be experienced
Does not apply to me

The more distance I keep away from her
The more I want to be around her
And the more love I feel for her
Something always tells me to go to her

LOVE IS MISERABLE

I always try to do something next to her
Just so she can say something

She always does
Because she also wants me around her
She enjoys my company
By just looking at her
Makes me feel good
But deep inside my heart

I feel a lot of pain
Painkillers cannot cure the pain
Only her can
I can't stop thinking about her
I just can't keep away from her
Because I so much love her

RAPHALA MH©

LOVE IS JOYOUS

I FEEL BAD

I really feel bad for letting you go
Before I could have you
I feel bad for letting you destroy
What we could have built
Before we even laid the foundation

Perhaps if I had stopped you
We could have constructed a mansion
I feel very bad for letting you destroy
My feelings for you before you could feel them
I feel bad for letting you delay

And later deny us a chance
Perhaps if I had stopped you
We would be the happiest couple
I feel bad for letting you
Keep a short distance apart

Because it feels like
It is a million miles distance
But you left me no choice
Only if you had given me a chance
Not to prove myself

But to love you even more
You knew how much I loved you
Yet you denied me a chance
You made me beg a lot from you
But that didn't pay off well

You made me love you more
By playing hard to get

But it was the hardest on earth
And no man could ever stand it
Despite how much he loves you

I have been endurance and patient
But you pinned more pain on me
Only if you had given me a chance
We would probably now be happier
But you chose to make an otherwise decision

RAPHALA MH©

WHY CAN'T

Why can't I stop my painful tears
When your name cross my imaginations
Why can't I stop missing you
And kill all my feelings for you
Why can't I just forget about you instead

And stop thinking of you frequently
Why can't I stop loving you
Why won't your smile stop appeasing me
Why can't the pain stop instantly
That is tearing my heart into pieces

Why can't I really stop the feelings
When they get stronger
Why do they develop even more
Why can't my heart stop bleeding
Over and over again

Every time I think of you
A brand new unbearable pain develops
Why can't I stop being a fool
For loving you in fantasy
When deep down

I know that you are not even mine
Why can't I stop hurting myself
Even when I can't bear the pain
Why can't I let go
Even when I am suffering

It is because I love you
I wish I could describe how

LOVE IS MISERABLE

But my mind goes blank
Then I run out of words
Like a thief caught on action

And my tongue chickens out
Yet one thing I do know
Is that I will never stop loving you
No matter how you feel about me
Your negative reply is motivation to me

And your positive reply is medication
To my hurting heart
That burns every second with love
I love you very much my dear
That is my only priority

RAPHALA MH©

MADE TO LOVE YOU

There is one thing that surprises me
I have no power in deciding who to love
But something lets me love you only
It is more like a gene in me of loving one person
I don't know why I love you so much
But there is this element in me

That allows me to really love you
And it also intercepts
My love for you to deteriorate
People have tried to interpret my love for you
But they failed to understand it
You also tried to interpret it

But it confuses you
I too, also tried to interpret it
But I am failing to reach a reliable solution
Instead I get new and special developments daily
Let's summarize it by saying
You are an extra ordinary person

Who is being loved extra ordinarily
Whenever I see a girl, I see you in her
Whenever I talk to a girl
I hear her speaking with your voice
Always when I see a beautiful creature
It reflects your image

I fail to see the beauty of other women
Because I am blinded by yours
I fail to feel the presence
Of other women in my life

LOVE IS MISERABLE

Because all my senses
Are full of your magic touch

When you talk to me
I stare at you deep inside your eyes
And I hear only a few words you say
Yet I am listening
Because you are beautiful
And your charming eyes occupy my thinking

I am loving you the way
A man can never imagine
I love you more every day
If there was a love gauge
I would use it to measure
How much love I am developing

For you daily
The fact that I cannot love anyone
But you, and only you
Tells me that I was made to love you
You are specially made
To be really loved by me

It seems like loving you
Is the mission God
Brought me on earth to accomplish
I truly love you
Because I was made to love you
And I will serve my purpose

RAPHALA MH©

LOVE IS JOYOUS

BECAUSE OF ME

If it is all because of me
Or all because I love you
That you have to go through
So much pain
And so much suffer

Having depressed emotions
Feelings crushing inside you
Having to altercate
With yourself daily
Your heart becoming more

Confused day by day
Taking decisions with confidence
And switching to opposite ones
Contradicting what your heart desires
Going for what you think

It is right for your heart
Then be unsure later
Failing to decide
What is best for you
Then I shall compromise

And withdraw my proposal
But I won't stop loving you
I will just do what you desire
Sacrificing my love
Just to make you happy

Is not a priority to me
It is not because I am not serious

LOVE IS MISERABLE

Nor I am too generous
But the truth is
I truly love you

And I am ready
To lose anything
Just to see you happy
That much I love you
And it will never change

RAPHALA MH©

LOVE IS MISERABLE

SONNETS

DAY DREAMING

I found myself screaming
But I was in fact dreaming
Having a scary but nice dream
Altercating with thugs in dreams
For the woman of my dreams
Before I could wake up
I tried to stand up
They shot me to death
But I was not yet dead
They tried to steal
But I put them to stop
Before I could even realize
The property was released
Out of the dreams I was released

RAPHALA MH©

THINKING ABOUT HER

I am thinking about not anyone
But about a special someone
The most glittering sunshine
Brighter than when the stars shine
She is not beautiful herself
But she defines beauty itself
Her presence feels pleasant
Because she is God sent
She is worthy of my thoughts
Because her beauty is thoughtful
She is not really perfect
But she is perfect in her imperfections
She deserves not complaints
But only complements

RAPHALA MH©

SHE FEELS NEGLECTED

She feels neglected
Yet she is the one who neglects
She kept a distance
Unaware that it was the greatest distance
The affection is less
Yet she is not loved less
I have seen it myself
She is destroying herself
She fails to talk about it
Although it is the only solution for it
She will talk when she is ready
Because I am ready, already
If she knows what she need
She will get what she seeks

RAPHALA MH©

YOU ARE NOT ALONE

You have been through hell
But all will be well
I could see how much you are hurting
It feels like I am the one who is hurting
I am not with you on sympathy
But fully with empathy
You can't go down the lane alone
Because you are not alone
I can't help you cry
But I can stop you to cry
You've had it all so hard
But don't let it break your heart
Don't let it make you lonely
Because you are really not alone

RAPHALA MH ©

HER EMOTIONS

Her emotions are not ordinary
They make her think informally
They make her hate love
For she fears real love
She believes in loyalty
But also fears full loyalty
Because it broke her heart
Yet it is her loyalty that hit her hard
Her love history blindfolds her
For her ex-boyfriends hurt her
She fails to recognize real love
Because she was hurt by her real love
Love makes her very emotional
Hence she becomes driven by emotions

RAPHALA MH ©

LOVE IS MISERABLE

FEARING LOVE

I want to be loved
But I am shy to be laughed
I used to love very hard
But love destroyed my heart
It took me much to earn trust
But it took me very little to not trust
I fail to fall in real love
Yet I know I am really loved
I want you to be mine
But I fear to be hurt by what is mine
I have fallen for you already
I want to be with you, but I am not ready
I really wish to be in love
But I fear real love

RAPHALA MH ©

WE ARE HURT

She does not like being hurt
Her heart is broken into pieces
Thus she is deeply hurt
She fails to break the pain into pieces
I could support her with sympathy
But my heart too is broken
I am thus with her with empathy
Trying to put together what is broken
All pains are caused by love
It hit us not smooth
Yet, we should be comforted by love
Because of it, our hearts should sooth
We experienced love harshly
For we had it roughly

RAPHALA MH ©

DEPRESSED BY LOVE

I am feeling very depressed
But actually I am compressed
Deep inside my heart
And I feel like I am hurt
I don't want to be laughed
But I want to love
I fear to express myself
Because I end up hurting myself
All those that I loved
Are now other people's lovers
I failed to be with them
Yet other men got them
My intention is not to impress
But I fail just to express

RAPHALA MH ©

FOREVER LOVE YOU

Every morning I wake up
I think much of you
I tried to give up
And forget about you
But it becomes worse
Day in day out
Sometimes I feel like I am cursed
I wish I could burst out
Whatever that prevents
You and I to be together
I tried but I can't pretend
I promise I will love you forever
For as long as you wish
Because love always wins

RAPHALA MH ©

HUNGER OF LOVE

I have been hurt
A donkey times
There are holes in my heart
Which I tried to patch many times
But love does not adore me
It really hates me
I do not have anger issues
But love makes me angry
That I cannot even solve my issues
Although I am hungry
Love is compressed inside me
I am feeling very lonely
I need to feed my feelings
By expressing my love and not a fling

RAPHALA MH©

LOVE ME FOR WHO I AM

Love me for who I am
Not for them
Share the love with me
Not with them
Be who you are
Not who they think you are
I highly value your presence
Because it is like a present
Be my super woman
I will be your super man
Be my super heroin
I will be your super hero
Live forever in my heart
I will forever live in your heart

RAPHALA MH©

WELL AWARE

I am well aware that I love her
And I also know that she is taken
But that does not destroy my love for her
I wish I had the powers to take
Her away from her lover
But I would be a jerk
And not a true lover
I cannot let her date a perk
Of men because I love her
I made peace with my feelings for her
We agreed to part ways
But my heart opposes the agreement
It deals with things on its own way
Regardless of disappointments

RAPHALA MH©

TIRED OF LOVE

I am extremely tired
Of fighting for love
And get hurt in return
Then people have a reason to laugh
I have a deep wound
That is cut through my heart
It is like a hole
Filled with depressions that hurt
My entire loving capacities
I lost hope on love
There are great possibilities
That I might never fall in love
Ever again in my life
Because it ruined my life

RAPHALA MH©

I KNOW YOU CAN

I know you can
Take care of my feelings
And contain them in a can
Where I will really feel
That I am loved
By not just anyone
Because not everyone can really love
But by an extraordinary someone
Whom her affection
Does not degrade
It does not have side effects
To our love, as it upgrades
Up to the highest level
Where our love, will advance to climax

RAPHALA MH ©

WE BELONG TOGETHER

We appear to have a greater bond
Explained in a bold font
Storms and winds can destroy everything
But to us they are nothing
Life sometimes becomes a mess
Through all the sorrows we are endurance
Because the love we have is not less
For us, real love is insurance
Our love is fixed by the Lord
For no one can ever be able to break
Because we love each other a lot
The affection between us is not fake
We will forever go stronger
Until the Lord feels it's longer

RAPHALA MH©

LOVE IS MISERABLE

SUNSHINE

Can you be my sunshine
Not up in the sky
Like when the stars shine
At night in the sky
But deep in my heart
Where I will feel warm
And never be hurt
Hence alleviating all the storms
Occupy the entire space
Just so no intruder will have access
To fill up the left space
Then our love will be a success
A couple people will adore
We shall be forever more

RAPHALA MH©

LET THERE BE LOVE

Let there be love
Shared amongst us
Let us all feel love
They should be loved by us
Let us set our hearts free
To accept being loved
And be loved freely
So that we can also freely love
For love should be real
Not a playground
Hence we must love in reality
Not in fantasy grounds
We must fully express
And love with exemption

RAPHALA MH©

LOVE IS MISERABLE

LOVE IS UNCONSCIOUS

It happens unconsciously
When you fall in love
If it happens consciously
Know that it is not real love
It can rather be lust
That temporarily fools your feelings
It does not come from your heart
It is a kind of a feeling
That lies to your mind
And all your loving particles
A possibility is that it might
Become a definite article
That you will get hurt
And falsely blame your heart

RAPHALA MH©

FELL FOR THE TRAP

Spoken with a soft voice
Enough to convince like a serpent
The words were pure, non-dull non void
I don't know why she was nice
But all serpents have that character
I felt my heart melting
Love was flowing like a narrator
Very fast my heart was beating
Little did I know
That it was all an act
How could I have said no
When all seemed like facts
I fell easily on the trap
Unfortunately I was left a scrap

RAPHALA MH©

LOVE IS MISERABLE

LOVE GONE TO WASTE

Words once were breakfast
When I first met you
But everything vanished so fast
When I think about you
Tears flow down my cheeks
With no one to wipe them
From days to weeks
Then to months and years
I have been waiting
For someone so special
I thought I was investing
My love for you very specially
But all has gone to waste
Because my love has lost weight

RAPHALA MH©

TAKEN AWAY

I know she loved me
And I loved her
She never told me
But I could see through her
There was no need to confess
I was just confused
Everything was a mess
She also got confused
Right under my nose
She was taken
I could not make noise
Because I was awakened
When everything happened
The pain in my heart is deepened

RAPHALA MH©

LOST HER

I fooled myself
I was a fool in love
She expressed herself
Fully like a loving dove
I failed to see that beauty
I thought I was in control
Yet I failed to express inner beauty
Because pride was in control
I knew I loved her
But I was blind to see her love
Now that I have lost her
I wish I could blame it on love
But I blame my foolishness
Together with my blindness

RAPHALA MH©

FEEL LIKE

I feel like I don't care
I feel like I am done
I tried to show her that I care
Because I thought she was the one
But she has told me straight
That I should stop bluffing
And I should start thinking straight
She and I will never be anything
It doesn't matter if I love her
Whether I am hurt or not
Maybe I should stop thinking about her
And tell myself to worry not
That to me she was attached
Except that she has to be detached

RAPHALA MH©

THREAT CONTACT

It happened suddenly that
Our contact is a threat
I wish she had thought that
My love is of no absolute threat
To her and her relationship
I don't want to break her
My heart desires more that friendship
Not with anyone if not her
Do not contact me anymore
She said to me confidently
She forgot that I love her more
But I am a threat apparently
My love to her no longer matters
And things are getting no better

RAPHALA MH©

WE DEFINE TRUE LOVE

Many people believe that love is extinct
They think they know the real story
But there are hidden distinct
Behind the whole story
Love is a complex world
It requires tolerance
Hence, it can be destroyed by words
But to us love is assurance
I promise to love you
Until my heart stops beating
I know I was made for you
That's why our love is always winning
We were made to be
And we shall remain together like bees

RAPHALA MH©

LOVE IS MISERABLE

TRIBUTE TO MY LATE FATHER

RAPHALA MH©

LOVE IS JOYOUS

P
PURE
PAGE
PRES.

FACEBOOK: PURE PAGE PRES

AND/OR

SECRET LINES POETRY

THANKS FOR READING

CONNECT WITH THE

AUTHOR

ON

Facebook: Raphala Mahuna Lekhosi

Twitter: @Raphalamh194

Instagram: Raphala Mahuna

Call/Whatsapp: 0827603194

Email: raphalamh@gmail.com

LOVE IS MISERABLE

LOVE IS JOYOUS

www.ingramcontent.com/pod-product-compliance
Lightning Source LLC
Chambersburg PA
CBHW021206020426
42331CB00003B/221